Desert
Dreamings

Deirdre Stokes

Heinemann
LIBRARY
Harcourt Education

First published in 2004 by Heinemann Library
a division of Harcourt Education Australia,
18–22 Salmon Street, Port Melbourne Victoria 3207 Australia
(a division of Reed International Books Australia Pty Ltd, ABN 70 001 002 357).
Visit the Heinemann Library website @ www.heinemannlibrary.com.au

ℛ A Reed Elsevier company

Editorial: Michelle Freeman, Carmel Heron
Cover and text design: Stella Vassiliou, Marta White, Kerri Wilson
Picture research: Wendy Duncan
Production: Tracey Jarrett

Typeset in 12.5/17pt Sabon
Pre-press by Digital Imaging Group (DIG)
Printed in China by WKT Company Ltd.

The paper used to print this book comes from sustainable resources.

National Library of Australia Cataloguing-in-Publication data:

Stokes, Deirdre.
    Desert dreamings.

    New ed.
    Includes Index.
    For primary and secondary school students.
    ISBN 1 74070 224 7.

    1. Art, Aboriginal Australian – Juvenile literature.
    I. Title. (Series : Australian library (Port Melbourne, Vic.)).

759.994

Acknowledgements

The publisher would like to thank Dr Zane Ma Rhea for her assistance.

The publisher would like to thank the following for permission to reproduce photographs: Aboriginal Artists Agency Sydney: pp. **10, 20, 24, 25**; AIATSIS: p. **17**; ANT Photo Library: p. **30** (left), /J. Burt: p. **18** (lower left); /Denis & Theresa O'Byrne: pp. **9** (bottom), **12**; /Otto Rogge: pp. **6, 18** (top), **30** (right); APL/Charles Lenars: p. **8**, /Paul A. Souders: p. **5**, /John Van Hasselt: pp. **16, 19** (bottom left); APL/Corbis: p. **15**, /Penny Tweedie: p. **9** (top); Art Gallery of NSW and Aboriginal Artists Agency Sydney: p. **14**; Australian Museum, Sydney: p. **13**; Les Gilliland: pp. **18** (lower right), **19** (top and middle); The Holmes à Court Collection, Heytesbury Pty Ltd: p. **23** (both); Lonely Planet Images/ Richard l'Anson: p. **4**; reproduced with permission of the National Gallery of Victoria pp. **1, 21** (both), **26, 27**; George Chaloupka, NT Museum of Arts and Sciences: p. **7** (top); photolibrary.com/Ted Mead: p. **18** (middle), /Stefan Mokrzecki: pp. **19** (bottom right), **28**; Jimmy Pike: p. **22**; Skyscans/David Hancock: p. **7** (bottom); Wildlight/Philip Quirk: p. **29** (both).

Cover photograph of *Warlugulong* 1976, by Clifford Possum Tjapaltjarri and Tim Leura Tjapaltjarri, reproduced with permission of the Art Gallery of NSW and Aboriginal Artists Agency Sydney.

Contents

Words that are printed in bold, **like this**, are explained in the Glossary on page 31.

Aboriginal art

Art is an essential part of Aboriginal culture. It can reflect the close association between the people and their land, and is often used to tell **Dreaming** stories, which are at the heart of Indigenous spirituality and beliefs.

In recent times, Aboriginal art has become widely appreciated, but this has caused some problems for the artists. As Indigenous designs have become popular, they have sometimes been used without permission. However, **copyright laws** protect the rights of the artists, and penalise anyone who uses Indigenous designs without permission.

Today, people from all over the world are enjoying and purchasing Aboriginal art. Paintings and other types of artworks are displayed in public galleries and sold by art dealers all around the world.

The artworks of Aboriginal artists often reflect the harsh yet beautiful desert landscapes of the Northern Territory, South Australia and Western Australia.

Places such as the Bungle Bungle Range in Purnululu National Park, Western Australia, have special religious importance to the Aboriginal groups who come from the area.

Tjukurpa

Tjukurpa is an Anangu word that non-Aboriginals interpret as **Dreamtime**. To Anangu, *Tjukurpa* means existence in the past, present and future. Aboriginal people believe in a Creation time, or Dreamtime, when **Ancestral Beings** emerged from beneath the earth. They resembled plants and animals, but were part-human.

Journeying across the land, these **ancestors** created everything that formed the world. They behaved like human beings – hunting, fighting, loving and hating. They taught their descendants the sacred rituals and the symbols and designs used in body painting.

The Ancestral Beings were the law-makers and from their deeds Aboriginal people learnt the correct way to behave and to live with each other. But as they tired of their lives, the Ancestral Beings disappeared under the earth again. Such places are often marked by rocky outcrops and trees and have special religious significance to Aboriginal people.

Types of desert art

In the past, the **nomadic** way of life practised by Aboriginal groups in the desert, and the extremes of the desert climate, made it difficult to preserve artworks for a long time. Designs painted on **artefacts** quickly wore off. Body paint and sand **mosaics** were only intended to last for the duration of the ceremony.

Today, however, great care is taken to preserve and record Aboriginal art. It is recognised as an important part of Indigenous and Australian heritage.

Rock engraving

Rock engraving is the oldest and most lasting form of traditional Aboriginal art and is found in most parts of Australia where there are suitable rock surfaces. Many different methods were used to cut into rock. These include rubbing, scratching, drilling and pitting. Stone, wooden or other **implements** were used, depending on the texture of the rock.

These rock engravings, about 100 km south of Alice Springs, are believed to be thousands of years old. They include circles, arcs, lines, and bird and animal tracks.

Rock painting

In the desert areas of Central and South Australia, designs used in rock painting are similar to those used in rock engraving.

Aboriginal artists used natural **pigments** – white from pipe clay or **gypsum**, red and yellow **ochres** from the earth and black from charcoal or **manganese**. The pigments were ground to a powder and mixed with a natural glue, then applied with the fingers or a brush. Brushes might be made from a chewed twig, strips of bark or human hair, depending on the type of surface to be covered.

Often, drawings were made with a small stone and then paint was rubbed on with the hand. Paint might also be splattered onto rock walls or a stencilled design made by blowing paint over an object such as a hand.

Places that display many pieces of rock art are called 'galleries', and some continue to be **spiritually** important to Aboriginal peoples today.

Sand drawings can depict objects, illustrate a story, or be a map of the landscape, indicating landmarks and distances to be travelled.

Sand drawings

Traditionally, storytelling is the way in which Aboriginal peoples preserve and pass on their history and religious knowledge. Sand drawings are often an important part of communication between the teller and the listener.

Types of desert art

Ground mosaics

Ground **mosaics** are made from the finely chopped leaves, stems and flowers of the native daisy and birds' feathers. The pulp is rubbed in animal fat. Half is then dyed with powdered yellow or red **ochre** or human blood, the other half with powdered white clay or black charcoal, and formed into small pellets.

A piece of ground is cleared and flattened, and spread with crumbled termite mound to give a hard working surface. The coloured pellets are placed side-by-side to create the design.

The mosaics are usually part of a religious ceremony. Sometimes they include a ceremonial pole in the centre. The mosaics are destroyed by the dancing during the ceremony. Only ground mosaics of a non-sacred nature can be photographed.

Traditionally, ground mosaics were hardly ever seen by people from outside the Aboriginal group who created them, because they were usually produced for sacred religious ceremonies.

Body painting

Body painting is a group activity associated with various ceremonies. The painting begins several hours before the ceremony and is accompanied by singing to call on the **spiritual** powers of the **Ancestral Beings**.

The body is first greased. Then the traditional designs are applied with the index finger and painting sticks. The materials used include red ochre, black charcoal and white clay.

These Western Desert men are applying body paint in preparation for a **corroboree**.

Painting on artefacts

Throughout the Western Desert there is an important tradition of woodcarving. For many generations, water carriers, spear-throwers, boomerangs and other **artefacts** have been superbly carved and painted. The designs used are similar to those in body decoration, ground mosaics and sand drawings.

Water carriers and other wooden artefacts are painted with designs that tell a story.

Hidden messages

Aboriginal art uses traditional symbols that can be read in many ways. Because of this, even the secret, sacred parts of a **Dreaming** can be painted but still remain hidden from non-Aboriginal viewers. The artist is the only person who fully understands the meaning.

Mary Dixon Nungurrayi
Warlpiri
Witchetty Grub Dreaming
92 cm x 76 cm

This painting is associated with the Witchetty Grub Dreaming site of Kunatjarrayi to the north-west of Papunya, in the Northern Territory. The painting depicts women, represented by 'U' shapes, using digging sticks and wooden bowls to gather witchetty grubs from the roots of trees. As they dig, one of the grubs turns into a snake and travels north towards the Granites, an important rock formation. At a deeper level, a **parallel** can be drawn between the witchetty grub turning into a moth and a boy's initiation into manhood.

Symbols of desert art

These are some of the traditional symbols used in desert art. They have many different **interpretations**; only a few of their meanings are given.

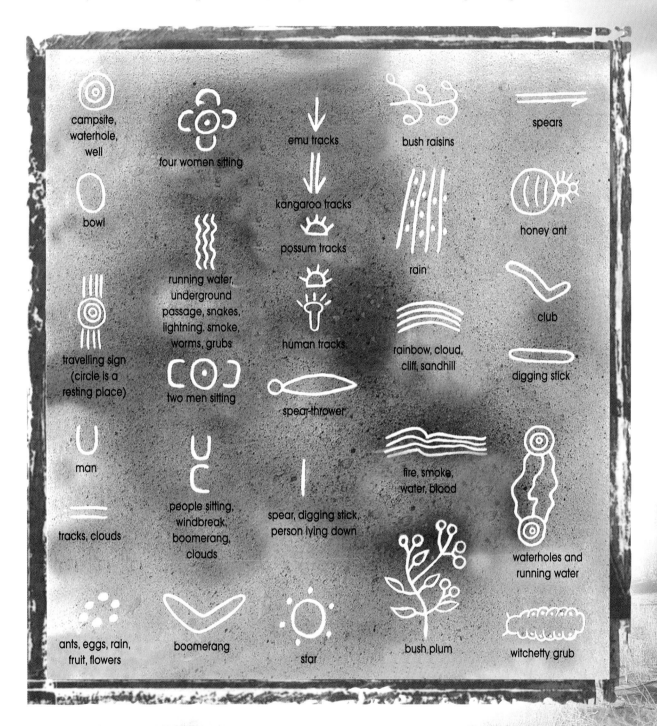

campsite, waterhole, well

four women sitting

emu tracks

bush raisins

spears

bowl

kangaroo tracks

possum tracks

rain

honey ant

running water, underground passage, snakes, lightning, smoke, worms, grubs

human tracks

rainbow, cloud, cliff, sandhill

club

travelling sign (circle is a resting place)

two men sitting

spear-thrower

digging stick

man

people sitting, windbreak, boomerang, clouds

spear, digging stick, person lying down

fire, smoke, water, blood

waterholes and running water

tracks, clouds

ants, eggs, rain, fruit, flowers

boomerang

star

bush plum

witchetty grub

Dots in Aboriginal art

The use of dots in modern Aboriginal paintings comes from rock painting, body painting and ground designs (sand drawings and ground **mosaics**). The coloured patterns of dots, side-by-side or dot-on-dot, create **three-dimensional** pictures full of life and movement.

In this modern painting, patterns of dots are used to represent a traditional food-gathering story. The women (who traditionally collect bush tucker) are shown by the 'U' shapes; the long thin shapes are the digging sticks; and the ovals are the wooden dishes in which the foods are placed.

Looking at desert art

Dots may also represent the landscape. When viewed from a high point or from the air, the country often appears dotted with low scrub, clumps of spinifex, trees, sandhills and rocky outcrops.

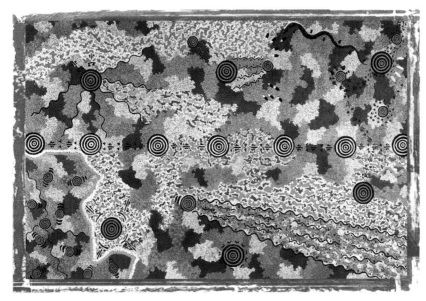

Michael Jagamarra Nelson
(born 1949)
Warlpiri (Papunya, NT)
Dreaming sites in the Western Desert

This painting depicts parts of the landscape in the Western Desert that are important to the Warlpiri people. A key has been provided to explain the meanings of different parts of the painting.

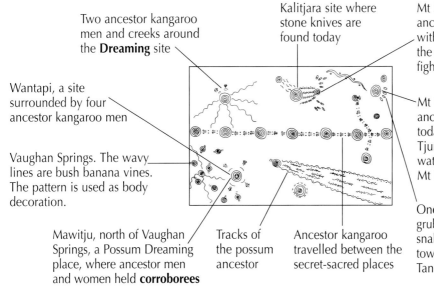

Two ancestor kangaroo men and creeks around the **Dreaming** site

Kalitjara site where stone knives are found today

Mt Singleton, where ancestor possum men armed with stone knives defeated the **ancestor** witchetty grubs fighting with wild potatoes

Wantapi, a site surrounded by four ancestor kangaroo men

Vaughan Springs. The wavy lines are bush banana vines. The pattern is used as body decoration.

Mt Wedge, where the ancestor wallaby still sits today after journeying from Tjuniyu, stopping at a waterhole before reaching Mt Wedge

Mawitju, north of Vaughan Springs, a Possum Dreaming place, where ancestor men and women held **corroborees**

Tracks of the possum ancestor

Ancestor kangaroo travelled between the secret-sacred places

One of the four witchetty grubs turned into a rainbow snake and travelled north towards the Granites in the Tanami Desert

Stories of the Dreamtime

The stories of the ancestral journeys tell about the landscape, animal habits, social laws and customs, and religious beliefs. The painting *Warlugulong* is like an aerial map of the artist's country, depicting the journeys of **Dreamtime ancestors** and teaching social law and custom.

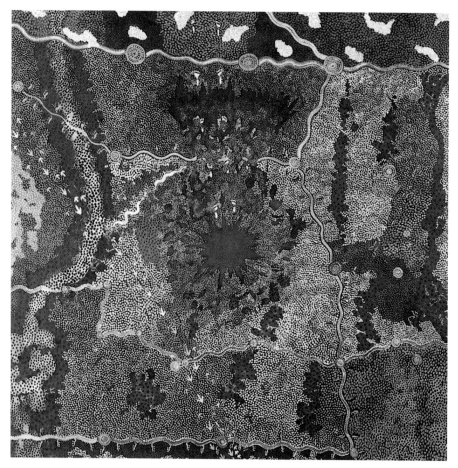

Clifford Possum Tjapaltjarri and Tim Leura Tjapaltjarri
Anmatyerre, Arrernte
Papunya, Alice Springs, NT
Warlugulong, 1976
synthetic polymer paint on canvas, 168.5 x 170.5 cm
Purchased 1981
Collection: Art Gallery of New South Wales
© Aboriginal Artists Agency Ltd
photograph: Christopher Snee for AGNSW

Lungkata the Blue-tongue Lizard Man

The central story of Tjapaltjarri's painting *Warlugulong* is of Lungkata the Blue-tongue Lizard Man, whose two sons speared a kangaroo while out hunting. Feeling very hungry, they decided to cook and eat it themselves, instead of sharing it with their father as the law demands.

Lungkata grew suspicious about their long absence and, when he realised what had happened, decided to punish them immediately for breaking the law. Blowing on his fire stick until it glowed, he set light to a dry bush that exploded into flame. Tongues of flame flicked out like the tongue of the blue-tongue lizard and raced across the land.

Very quickly the flames caught up with the two sons. They tried to beat out the flames with tree branches, but it was useless. However fast they ran, the fire followed them.

Finally exhausted, the brothers could run no longer and the flames overwhelmed them.

Desert artist Clifford Possum Tjapaljarri at work.

New materials, traditional stories

In the early 1970s, a new development in Aboriginal art took place at Papunya School, in the Northern Territory. Aboriginal students were encouraged to paint murals on the walls in their traditional designs, using **acrylic** paints. Acrylic paints are ideal for the hot, dusty, desert conditions. They only need to be thinned with water, they are quick-drying and permanent and can be applied with any kind of **implement**.

The children's work remained unfinished, but several of the older men in the community completed the project. Soon, many Aboriginal artists began to paint their **Dreamings** in acrylic paints on canvas or any available scrap material.

Pitjantjatjara artist William Sandy working on a canvas at Papunya. People from several different language groups live and work at Papunya.

Yuendumu

At Yuendumu, also in the Northern Territory, the older men then decided to paint their traditional stories on the school doors. The men felt that the children had no knowledge of Dreaming stories or traditional Aboriginal laws and customs, and that these important things could be taught through artworks.

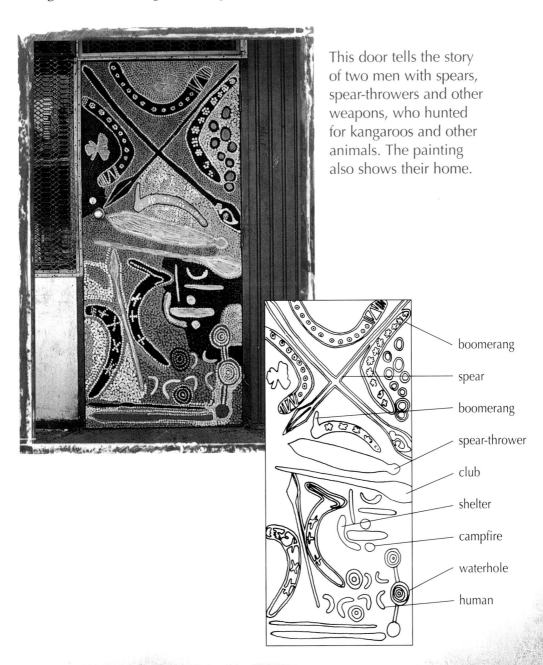

This door tells the story of two men with spears, spear-throwers and other weapons, who hunted for kangaroos and other animals. The painting also shows their home.

boomerang

spear

boomerang

spear-thrower

club

shelter

campfire

waterhole

human

Where desert artists live

Each group has its own lands. The features of the landscape and sacred sites created by **ancestors** are important in every aspect of life.

Great Sandy Desert

Many different language groups live in the East Kimberley and Great Sandy Desert of Western Australia. The artist Jimmy Pike was a Walmajarri man from the Great Sandy Desert.

Pintupi

Pintupi people live on the borders of Western Australia and the Northern Territory, in the Gibson Desert. Some of the first Indigenous artists to use **acrylic** paints come from this language group.

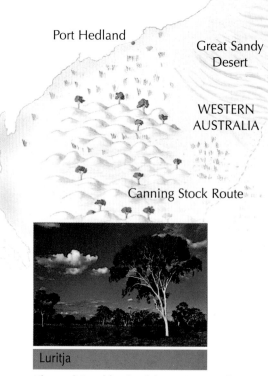

Broome

Port Hedland

Great Sandy Desert

WESTERN AUSTRALIA

Canning Stock Route

Warlpiri

Warlpiri people are from the desert areas north-west of Alice Springs in the Northern Territory. The art movement that originated at Yuendumu has become successful in the world of Indigenous art.

Luritja

The traditional lands of the Luritja people are found approximately 230 km west of Alice Springs. Since the founding of an arts centre in 1992, the community around Ikuntji (Haast's Bluff) has become well known for their paintings in acrylics.

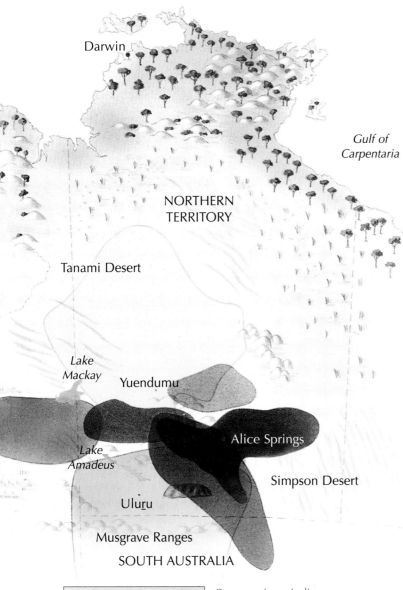

Darwin

Gulf of
Carpentaria

NORTHERN
TERRITORY

Tanami Desert

Lake
Mackay   Yuendumu

Lake
Amadeus

Alice Springs

Simpson Desert

Uluṟu

Musgrave Ranges

SOUTH AUSTRALIA

Arrernte

Arrernte people live in the
centre of Australia. They use art
and ceremonies to maintain and
protect many of their traditions.

Anmatyerre

Anmatyerre people come from a
desert area north of Alice Springs in
the Northern Territory. The famous
artist Clifford Possum Tjapaltjarri
was an Anmatyerre man.

Pitjanjatjara

Pitjanjatjara people are the
custodians of Uluṟu, and continue
to live a traditional lifestyle while
producing artworks such as
wooden **artefacts** for sale.

Papunya

Papunya is an Indigenous
settlement made up of desert
peoples from several different
language groups. The Papunya art
movement, started in 1971, has
produced successful artists such
as Michael Jagamarra Nelson.

The paintings, the land and the people

The paintings are a visual record of the **Dreamings**, and they explain the artist's relationship to the land. In the mind of the artist, the land is mapped out with Dreaming trails and the features created by the **ancestors**.

Artist Michael Jagamarra Nelson with one of his paintings. The painting reflects the colours and appearance of the landscape.

Storytelling

Canvases may be painted by one artist, by a husband and wife, or by a number of men or women of the same kinship group. As they paint, the artists sing the stories that explain the meanings of the symbols they are using.

Murtiyarru Sunfly Tjampitjin (Kukatja) c. 1916–1996
Tjikerri 1987
synthetic polymer paint on canvas
112 x 83 cm
Presented through The Art Foundation of Victoria
by Lauraine Diggins, Fellow, 1988
National Gallery of Victoria, Melbourne

Tjikerri is a sacred site for men. Warlayirti, the ancient leader of the Kukatja people, travelled to Tjikerri in the Dreaming. After a long journey from the north he lay down, forming the waterhole and lake shown at the top of the painting.

Peter Japanangka Blacksmith
(Kartangarruru) c. 1918–1991
Warna Jukurrpa (snake Dreaming) 1986
synthetic polymer paint and enamel
paint on composition board
110.6 x 202.3 cm
Purchased through The Art Foundation
of Victoria with the assistance of
CRA Limited, Fellow, 1989
National Gallery of Victoria, Melbourne

The painting tells the story of the powerful snake ancestor's journey in search of water. The snake's journey was followed by a rainbow, then rain.

Different places, different styles

The deep, personal bond between the artist and the land means that variations in the landscape have a strong influence on the style of the art. In the vast desert areas of northern and western Australia, the landscape varies considerably. This is reflected in the art.

These paintings are by artists living in different parts of the east Kimberley region in the north of Western Australia. Each has a distinctive way of depicting the landscape and the **Dreamings** associated with it.

Jimmy Pike (born c. 1940)
Walmajarri
Kurlku, Great Sandy Desert, WA
Yarntayi with jilji on both sides

Jimmy Pike was born and spent his childhood in the remote sandhill country of the Great Sandy Desert. His family lived a partly **nomadic** life moving from one waterhole to another within their own country. He is an expert at hunting and tracking, and knows every feature of the landscape.

This painting tells the **Dreamtime** story of the creation of Yarntayi. Two giant snakes travelled through the country, cutting a sinuous path from east to west. They pushed aside the *jilji* to leave wide, flat, treeless plains between them.

Rover Thomas's paintings are a visual record of the significance of the Kimberley landscape to the Aboriginal people. They include recent features such as roads, towns and cattle stations. This painting commemorates a massacre of Aboriginals that took place in the early days of European settlement.

Rover Thomas (born c. 1935)
Kukatja/Wangkajungka
Turkey Creek (Warnum, WA)
Bedford Downs Massacre, 1987
natural **pigments** and bush gum on cotton duck
89.5 cm x 180.5 cm

David Jarinyanu Downs (born c. 1925)
Wankajungu/Walmajarri
Fitzroy Crossing, WA
Kurtal as Miltjitauru, 1989
natural **ochres** and synthetic polymer on linen
183 cm x 122 cm

This painting explains the origin of a weather pattern that brings December rain storms to the Kimberleys in Western Australia. These storms, called **Miltjitauru**, signal the beginning of the wet season, and give relief from the stifling heat.

In this painting, Kurtal is depicted carrying the rain clouds and surrounded by them. Kurtal as *Miltjitauru* can destroy animals and people in his path, but he also creates life by making the dry soil **fertile** again.

A mixture of old and new

For thousands of years, desert Aboriginals have slept out under clear, star-studded skies. So it is not surprising that there are so many Creation stories explaining the origins of the Sun, Moon, stars and planets.

These two paintings by Warlpiri artists show contrasting techniques. Mary Dixon Nungurrayi uses traditional designs to depict a **Dreamtime** story. However, Aboriginal art is part of a living culture, and Bronson Nelson Jakamarra has introduced new symbols to help him depict a recent **astronomical** event.

In the Dreamtime seven young Aboriginal girls were looking for honey ants at Uluṟu. An old man, Jilbi, saw them and decided to steal two of them to become his wives. During the night he followed them across the desert, but to save them the Spirit Beings at Uluṟu put the seven girls into the sky to form the Seven Sister stars, also known as the Pleiades. Jilbi was put into the sky as the star Orion. He still continues his pursuit as he follows the sisters across the night sky.

The painting depicts the Seven Sisters, the stars of the night sky and the Milky Way. Surrounding these are the designs and the colours of the body painting worn by the women during a very important ceremony connected with this story.

Mary Dixon Nungurrayi
Warlpiri
Mt Liebig area, NT
The Seven Sisters Dreaming
synthetic polymer paint on canvas
128.5 cm x 83 cm

The artist was inspired by a technical drawing in a magazine illustrating the path of Halley's comet. The painting shows the comet at various stages as it circles the sun. The other planets, depicted as circles, are the Earth, the Moon, the Pleiades (Seven Sisters) and Venus. The white band is the Milky Way and the dots are the stars. The Milky Way and the Pleiades are important **Dreamings** for the Warlpiri people.

Bronson Nelson Jakamarra
Warlpiri
Yuendumu, NT
Halley's Comet, 1986
synthetic polymer paint on canvas
78 cm x 126 cm

Traditional medicine and art

Today, researchers are working to record age-old knowledge about medicinal plants. The healing properties of plants have been used by Indigenous peoples for thousands of years. Indigenous peoples have many traditions associated with healing plants, and these plants are often a subject of artworks.

Mick Namarari Tjapaltjarri (Pintupi) c. 1926–1998
Yam spirit Dreaming for children 1972
synthetic polymer paint on canvas
76.3 x 61.1 cm
Presented through The Art Foundation
of Victoria with the generous assistance of
North Broken Hill Limited, Fellow, 1987
National Gallery of Victoria, Melbourne

Tjapaltjarri painted this 'medicine story' because of his concerns for the health of the young Pintupi men. It was the first canvas painted at Papunya, in the Northern Territory, and was inspired by the need to teach the young men the traditional ways to enjoy good, healthy living.

The painting depicts four **corroboree** men dancing and chanting to 'keep the kids alive'. Above them is a large plant spreading across the desert, above it two 'kids alive'. In the lower sections of the painting, the roots of nutritious bush tucker can be seen pushing through the earth.

There is much ritual concerned with the collecting of plants for medicines, with special **Dreamings** to be sung to ensure the maximum medicinal value from the plants. The artist has depicted the whole medicine vine, with its roots, stem, leaves, flowers and fruit. The woody stem curls around the trunks and branches of trees like a huge snake. It has creamy-white flowers, and the fruit is green, ripening to red.

This plant is a commonly used and effective bush medicine. The heated leaves draw poison from infected sores, relieve headaches when placed on the forehead, and cure a sore throat when chewed. The stem, when softened and pounded, makes a sticky bandage.

Kumanjayi Napaljari (Warlpiri) c. 1926–2001
Ngalyipi Jukurrpa (medicine vine Dreaming) 1987
synthetic polymer paint on canvas
126.0 x 74.0 cm irreg.
Presented through The Art Foundation of Victoria by
Lauraine Diggins, Fellow, 1988
National Gallery of Victoria, Melbourne

Desert art in the city

Aboriginal art can now be seen in Australia's capital city, Canberra, in a form in which it is both useful and permanent.

The granite **mosaic** pavement in the open forecourt of Parliament House was designed by Michael Jagamarra Nelson. It represents the ancient continent of Australia and Australia's oldest civilisation.

The Aboriginal meaning of the name 'Canberra' is 'meeting place', and the mosaic shows a gathering of tribespeople of the Dingo, Wallaby and Goanna **ancestors** for an important ceremony.

During the construction, Nelson worked with the **mosaicists** to make sure that his **acrylic** painting was accurately transformed into the final mosaic.

The design was marked out on large sheets of paper, and the **setts** – small roughly-finished pieces of granite – were stuck in place on the paper (see photo at left). The setts were put in place by turning over the complete sheets. They were then cemented down and set in a background of black mortar (see photo below).

Wood art today

For thousands of years, Aboriginal peoples have been making useful **implements** from natural materials around them. These objects are often beautiful as well as useful. Traditionally, Aboriginal wooden objects were intended for everyday use, such as carrying water or hunting, not as decorative items. However, because of the beauty of these objects, many items are now on display in museums and galleries where people can view them.

Many Aboriginal settlements have arts and crafts centres, where locally made craftwork can be distributed and sold throughout Australia. This industry ensures that traditional skills are not lost, and provides income for craftspeople and their families.

These beautifully crafted wooden **artefacts** were made by Aboriginal people from the Northern Territory. The coolamons (left), or carrying dishes, have been decorated with hot **pokerwork** designs. The music sticks (right) are painted with designs taken from sand drawings, which in turn often depict events from the **Dreamings**.

Glossary

acrylic   quick-drying, synthetic paint

Ancestral Being (ancestor) according to Aboriginal religion, Ancestral Beings were ancient Spirit Beings who created the world and everything in it

artefact   human-made object

astronomical   to do with the stars and planets

copyright law   law that recognises the right of the creator of an artwork to have control over how and by who the artwork is used

corroboree   English version of a word used to describe Indigenous ceremonies. However, each Aboriginal language group has its own word to describe such ceremonies.

Dreaming   stories of the Creation. Dreamings can be told in many ways, including through paintings, dance and oral stories.

Dreamtime   Creation time, the time when Ancestral Beings roamed the land, creating the world we see today

fertile   producing healthy plant life

gypsum   soft, white mineral, easy to crush

implement   tool

interpretation   explanation

jilji   Walmajarri word meaning sandhills

manganese   hard, greyish-white mineral

Miltjitauru   Walmajarri word describing the storms that occur in the Kimberleys, Western Australia, each year in December

mosaic   arrangement of stones, glass or other natural materials that makes a picture

mosaicist   artist who creates mosaics

nomad   member of a group who chooses not to have a permanent home, and instead move from place to place in search of food

ochre   coloured clay used for body painting in Aboriginal religious ceremonies and other types of artworks

parallel   something that is very similar to another thing

pigment   colour

pokerwork   design burned into wood using a hot point, such as a wooden or metal stick

sett   small piece of granite, used in a mosaic

spiritual   to do with religious beliefs

three-dimensional   appearing solid instead of flat

Tjukurpa   Anangu word meaning existence in the past, present and future, sometimes used to describe the Dreamtime

index

A tutta la scuola elementare di Auchterhouse
J.D.

Il libro è stato precedentemente
pubblicato con il titolo *A spasso col mostro*

Traduzione di Laura Pelaschiar

Seconda edizione, marzo 2014

Titolo originale: *The Gruffalo*

Prima pubblicazione 1999, Macmillan Children's Books, Londra

Stampato in Belgio

ISBN 978-88-6714-263-7

IL GRUFFALÒ

Julia Donaldson
Illustrato da Axel Scheffler

EMME EDIZIONI

Un giorno un topino allegro e gioioso
andò a passeggiare nel bosco frondoso.
La volpe lo vide: «*Che buon bocconcino!*»
pensò, osservando il bel topolino.
– *Ciao topo, lo sai, la foresta è insidiosa...*
dài, vieni da me che ti offro qualcosa! –
– Sei molto gentile, ma dico di no:
mi vedo per cena con
il Gruffalò –.

La volpe gli chiese: – *E chi sarà mai?* –
– Ma come, davvero tu non lo sai?

Ha zanne tremende,

artigli affilati,

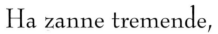

e denti da mostro di bava bagnati –.

– *E dove lo incontri?* –
– Accanto alla roccia dall'acqua lisciata...
...E a cena divora volpe impanata! –

– Volpe impanata? Ehm... ho da fare! –
E la volpe sparí senza farsi pregare.

– Che volpe sciocca, pensate un po':
crede che esista il Gruffalò! –

Avanti andò il topo e incontrò la civetta,
che scese dall'albero senza gran fretta.
L'uccello pensò: «*Ma che dolce spuntino!*»
e senza indugiare si fece vicino.
– *Ciao topo, di' un po', stasera sei solo?*
Ti va una cenetta... da prendere al volo? –
– Sei molto ospitale, ma sono impegnato:
dal Gruffalò a cena son
stato invitato –.

L'uccello gli chiese: – *E chi sarà mai?* –
– Ma come, davvero tu non lo sai?

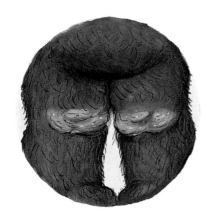

Ha ginocchia nodose   e terribili unghione

e un bitorzolo verde in cima al nasone –.

– *E dove lo incontri?* –
– Qui in riva al fiume...
Ah... e mangia civette con tutte le piume! –

– *Con tutte le piume?* – tremò la civetta,
e… vuum! volò via come una saetta.

– Stolido uccello, e gran credulone!
Il Gruffalò è solo una mia invenzione! –

Avanti andò il topo nel bosco frondoso,
contento, felice, allegro e gioioso.
Un grigio serpente sbucò tra l'erbetta:
«Ma guarda quel topo...» pensò «che cenetta!»
– Ehi, topo, che fai solo nella foresta?
Dài vieni da me, che facciamo una festa! –
– Sei molto gentile, ma dico di no.
Mi incontro per cena con il Gruffalò –.

– Con il Gruffalò? – chiese. – E chi sarà mai? –
– Ma come, davvero tu non lo sai?

Ha occhi arancioni,   la lingua molliccia,

e aculei violacei sulla pelliccia –.

– *E dove lo incontri?* –
– Qui in riva al laghetto…
Ah! E adora i serpenti cotti al funghetto –.

– Serpenti al funghetto? Per dindirindina! –
E scivolò via tra l'erba fina.

– Che sciocca la biscia! Nemmeno si sogna
che il Gruffalò è solo una bella menzogna… –

– ...Oh-oh! –

Ma ecco che il topo, non molto lontano,
si trova davanti un tipo un po' strano,
con zanne tremende e artigli affilati,
e denti da mostro di bava bagnati,
ginocchia nodose e terribili unghione,
e un bitorzolo verde in cima al nasone!
E occhi arancioni, e lingua molliccia...
e aculei violacei sulla pelliccia!

– Aiuto aiuto, si salvi chi può!
Ma allora esiste il Gruffalò! –

Il mostro esclamò: – *Ehi topo... ho fame!*
Saresti assai buono mangiato col pane –.

– Ti sbagli, mio caro. Io son la creatura
di cui tutti quanti qui hanno paura.
Lo so che non sembra, ma non è una bugia:
appena mi vedono, scappano via!

E se non ci credi, vieni con me –.
– *Okay*, – disse il Gruffalò, ridendo tra sé.

Avanzarono i due nella foresta ombrosa,
finché il Gruffalò disse: – *Ehi, sento qualcosa!* –

Li vide il serpente e rimase di stucco,
gli sussurrò il topo: – ...E non c'è trucco! –
– *Corbezzoli, è vero!* – esclamò la biscia,
e scivolò via tra l'erba liscia.

Il Gruffalò fece: – *Ma è stupefacente!* –
E il topo rispose: – Non sono uno che mente! –

Camminarono i due, senza gran fretta,
poi il Gruffalò disse: – *Toh, una civetta!* –

L'uccello li vide e rimase di stucco:
ecco lí il Gruffalò, e non c'era trucco!
– Civetta, sei tu! – la salutò il topo.
– *Ciao ciao, caro amico… vediamoci dopo!* –

– *Han tutti paura!* – disse il mostro interdetto.
E il topo rispose: – Te l'avevo pur detto –.

Andarono avanti tra l'erba e tra i sassi,
poi il Gruffalò disse: – *Mmmh, sento dei passi* –.

La volpe li vide e rimase di stucco:
un Gruffalò vero, non era un trucco!
– *Addio caro topo!* – d'un fiato esclamò
e in fondo alla tana se ne scappò.

Il topo concluse: – Lo vedi da te!
Qui attorno han tutti paura di me.
Ma ora mi sa che ho una gran fame...
che voglia di Gruffalò col salame! –

– *Gruffalò hai detto? Ehm, scusa, ho un impegno...* –
E via scappò il mostro, senza ritegno.

Tra i fiori e le foglie e gli aghi di pino
si siede felice il bel topolino.
Poi trova una ghianda... «Mmhhh, è squisita!
Che bella giornata! Che dolce è la vita!»